THE GOLDEN HORDE AND THE RISE OF MOSCOW

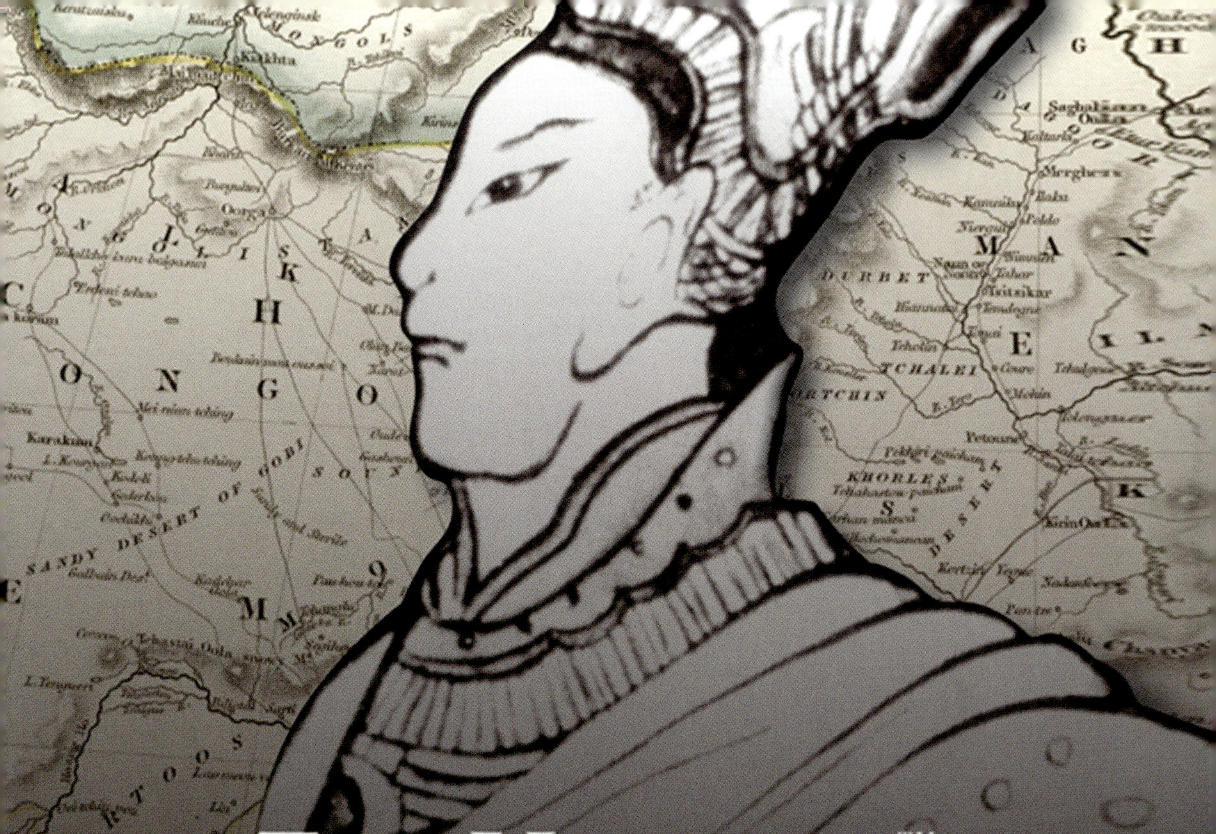

ns

THE MONGOLS™
THE GOLDEN HORDE AND THE RISE OF MOSCOW

ANN BYERS

New York

Published in 2017 by The Rosen Publishing Group, Inc.
29 East 21st Street, New York, NY 10010

Copyright © 2017 by The Rosen Publishing Group, Inc.

First Edition

All rights reserved. No part of this book may be reproduced in any form without permission in writing from the publisher, except by a reviewer.

Library of Congress Cataloging-in-Publication Data

Names: Byers, Ann, author.
Title: The Golden Horde and the rise of Moscow / Ann Byers.
Description: First edition. | New York : Rosen Publishing, 2017. | Series: The Mongols | Includes bibliographical references and index.
Identifiers: LCCN 2015049669 | ISBN 9781499463644 (library bound) | ISBN 9781499463620 (pbk.) | ISBN 9781499463637 (6-pack)
Subjects: LCSH: Golden Horde--History. | Kievan Rus--History--Mongol Invasion, 1237-1241. | Mongols--Russia--History. | Russia--History--1237-1480. | Moscow (Russia)--History--13th century.
Classification: LCC DS22.7 .B94 2016 | DDC 947/.03--dc23
LC record available at http://lccn.loc.gov/2015049669

Manufactured in China

Contents

Introduction..6

Chapter 1
Empire of Tents: The Mongols..............................9

Chapter 2
Empire of Cities: The Rus....................................16

Chapter 3
The Empires Clash...28

Chapter 4
A Winner Emerges..36

Chapter 5
A New Empire...48

Glossary..55

For More Information...57

For Further Reading...60

Bibliography..61

Index...62

Introduction

In the heart of the Eurasian continent, on the vast plains that join Europe to Asia, the 1200s were a tumultuous, violent century. One reason for the turmoil is the geography of the area, called the steppes. Steppe is the name for a huge swath of grassland stretching from present-day Romania in Eastern Europe to Manchuria in Asia. It is 5,000 miles (8,047 kilometers) from east to west and 200 to 600 miles (322 to 966 km) from north to south. The massive plain is divided by the Altai Mountains into two parts, the western and eastern steppes.

The climate of the steppes, especially the eastern steppe, is harsher than nearly every other place on earth. Summers are extremely hot—the Gobi Desert is southeast of the eastern steppe. Winters are bitter cold—the frozen tundra of Siberia is just north of much of the steppes. Very little rain falls. Because of the severe temperatures and the dry soil, almost the only vegetation on the steppes is grass. Some trees grow along the rivers and streams that cross the grasslands and in the mountains to the north of the western steppe, but the weather is too harsh and the soil too dry for food crops.

So the only way to survive on the steppes in the thirteenth century was to tend the animals that fed on the grasses—mainly sheep, goats, horses, and yaks. That meant living as nomads, following the herds. The people of the steppes were tribal or family groups living in herding camps they set up and took down as the animals moved from pasture to pasture. The groups were small, but there were many of them. They

Cousin to North American bison, yaks thrive on short steppe grasses. Mongols used their meat, milk, and fur and burned their dung for fuel.

traded in the villages or cities on the edges of the steppes, exchanging the hides, cheese, and meat from their animals for pottery, weapons, and other goods. They also did business with the caravans that came over the flat grasslands on the trading roads from Asia to Europe. When drought, disease among their animals, or other hardship struck and they had nothing to eat or trade, they resorted to raiding.

Competition among the different tribes for scarce resources often triggered violence. Any attack was met with retaliation, so inter-tribal warfare was a way of life on the steppes. Over the centuries, various groups banded together in confederations. At the beginning of the thirteenth century, a number of Turkic groups occupied the western steppe. In the east, a strong tribal leader began uniting the clans of his nomadic people into an alliance that would become a nation. The nation would grow into the Mongol Empire. It would span two continents and rule an estimated 100 million people at its peak.

The Mongol founder, Genghis Khan, divided rule of his empire among his four sons. The four divisions eventually developed into four separate kingdoms, called khanates. The army of the western khanate, which became known as the Golden Horde, pressed deep into what is now Russia and beyond, conquering one realm after another in areas that were geographically and culturally different from the steppes. At the height of its power, the Golden Horde ruled present-day Russia, Ukraine, Belarus, Kazakhstan, Moldova, and the Crimea. Its reign lasted more than two centuries.

Chapter 1
Empire of Tents: The Mongols

The Mongol Empire began as a confederation of nomadic tribes. These tribes roamed the eastern steppe, the area now called Mongolia, located north of modern China and east and south of Russia. As conflicts pitted the tribes against one another, a Mongol named Temujin emerged as a mighty warrior. Other Mongols joined him. His confederation grew as he defeated rival clans. When he won, he made the defeated soldiers part of his army and rewarded his followers. A smart leader as well as a good fighter, Temujin united the many Mongol clans. In 1206, the tribes acknowledged him as Genghis Khan, or Universal Ruler. The area he ruled was called a khanate.

With all of Mongolia firmly in his control, Genghis Khan set out to enlarge his khanate. He turned south and east, to what is now China, and west to Persia. In these places he did not strike nomad camps; he attacked cities. In and around cities were agricultural products, ceramic bowls, knives, silk fabrics, and other items the Mongols could not get on the steppe.

The people in the cities had not seen a force like the Mongols. They charged on horseback, controlling the horses with their legs as they fired deadly arrows. They were swift, sly, and savage. Within twenty years, Genghis Khan had conquered northern China, most of central Asia, and parts of the Middle East.

Without clay and other natural resources, Mongols could obtain items such as this ceramic oil lamp only by trading or raiding.

Cracks in the Empire

Such a large area was difficult to rule, but Genghis Khan was a good administrator. Before his death in 1227, he divided his vast land into four khanates: the territory that became the Yuan dynasty in the east (Mongolia and China), the Il-Khanate in the south (modern Iran), what later became known as the Khanate of the Golden Horde in the west (Russia and eastern Europe), and the Chagatai Khanate in the middle (central Asia). He gave the territories to his four sons as their inheritance. Each son was to be a khan, or ruler, and each was to have his own khanate.

But Genghis Khan did not want the empire split. He set up a system in which the four khanates were something like four states united together as one country. One of the four khans was to be the Great Khan, the ruler of the entire empire. He was to be elected at a kurultai, a meeting of Mongol clan leaders.

For people with a history of tribal warfare, deciding who would be the supreme leader by clan voting was a recipe for conflict. The first election was easy: Genghis Khan had chosen his third and favorite son, Ogedei, and he was easily voted the Great Khan. But after Ogedei's death in 1241, struggles for power led to disagreements, threats, murders, and wars among the brothers. By 1300, the Mongol Empire was no longer united; the four khanates had become four separate, independent kingdoms.

The People of the Felt Tents

Nomads who move every few months need mobile homes. The Mongol dwellings were circular tents called gers or, in Russian, yurts. A yurt was made of wood covered in felt. The sides, called khana, were lattices of crisscrossed poles. Several khana were tied together with strips of leather. From the places where the poles crossed, other poles were attached to form a domed roof. These poles were tied to a wooden ring at the top of the roof. The ring served as an opening for light, air, and smoke from the fire in the center of the yurt. The whole structure was covered in felt made from the wool of the herders' sheep, goats, or yaks.

Many Mongolians today choose to live in felt-covered yurts. However, today's yurts have wooden doors and iron stoves. Some have satellite dishes and solar panels.

The round shape, the sloping roof, and the thick felt protected the yurt from the harsh steppe winds. The door faced south because the Siberian winds came from the north.

The size of the tent depended on the number of khana used, which meant a yurt could be expanded as a family grew. Yurts could be quite large; Genghis Khan's was thirty feet (nine meters) in diameter. Yet typical yurts could be set up or disassembled in an hour and carried on three animals.

Because they were herders, the nomads had the wool for the felt and the leather for the ties. But no trees grew on the steppe, so they had to trade for the wood. Traders sold lightweight wood, ready-made poles, or completely manufactured khana. The traders, who lived on the edges of the steppe, called the Mongols the People of the Felt Tents.

THE GOLDEN HORDE

According to Mongol custom, the inheritance of the oldest son was the land farthest from his father's camp. Since Genghis Khan pitched his tents in the eastern khanate, he gave the westernmost portion of his territory to his oldest son. The oldest son died before his father, so his khanate was given to the son's two oldest children, Genghis Khan's grandsons. Orda, who agreed to let his younger brother rule, commanded the White Horde, and Batu was the leader of the Blue Horde.

"Horde," a word that comes from the Mongol for "camp," is the term for a large tribal group. The colors were probably

At its height, the Golden Horde occupied more than 2.3 million square miles (6 million square km). It stretched from eastern Europe into Siberia and controlled much of Russia.

Mongol associations with directions: white symbolized east, and blue stood for west. Later historians called the combined White and Blue Hordes the "Golden Horde." The name may have come from the color of Batu's tent, or it might be a term for "royal."

The Golden Horde is also sometimes called the Kipchak Khanate. The Kipchaks were a Turkic nomad group, one of the groups the Mongols conquered. When Batu became khan, he did not have a large army. Genghis Khan gave him only 4,000 of his 129,000 soldiers. As Batu defeated tribal groups, he assimilated them into his own. That is, they became part of the Golden Horde. Much of Batu's army was Kipchak, so people sometimes called the horde the Kipchak Khanate.

THE CONQUERING HORDE

As the grandson of the man who amassed more land than anyone before or since, Batu Khan knew how to invade and conquer. Shortly after Genghis Khan died, Batu helped his uncle Ogedei in his war against northern China. Ogedei, like his father, was bent on building the Mongol Empire. While he was busy claiming land in the east, he ordered the other khans to extend their territories also. For Batu, on the far edge of the empire, there was only one direction to go. He had to invade west, across the Ural Mountains … into the land of the Rus.

CHAPTER 2
EMPIRE OF CITIES: THE RUS

Even before Genghis Khan began forging the Mongol Empire on the steppes, another empire was growing. Across the Ural Mountains, northwest of the steppes, a people were uniting into a force that would challenge the domination of the Mongols. They called themselves the Rus.

The empire of the Rus developed very differently from that of the Mongols. The main reason was probably that its geography and climate are very different. The area that is now northwestern Russia is cool and dry, but not as cold and dry as the steppes. The northernmost part, sometimes called a snow forest, is thick with evergreens—pines, firs, and spruce. Going south, the temperatures are slightly warmer, and evergreens are mixed with other types of trees: oak, birch, and aspen. Unlike the steppes, northwestern Russia has a summer, although it is brief. The rains that fall during the summer allow some crops to grow.

SETTLED LIFESTYLE

The resources of the forests enabled the Rus to live settled lives instead of moving about as the people of the steppes were forced to do. The forests held many products. The trees provided lumber for houses, furnishings, and tools, as well as firewood. The trees also produced wax, and they were home

In the snow forests of the Ural Mountains, winters last at least six months. Temperatures in the very short summers average about 50°F (10°C).

to bees that made honey. One of the most important forest products was fur from bears, deer, squirrels, ermine, mink, and other animals. The Rus traded the wealth of the forests for the milk and cheese of the steppe nomads and the spices and handmade goods of the caravans that crossed their land.

The milder climate of northwestern Russia permitted some farming. Rye grew well in the cool weather, as did buckwheat and oats. So the people could grow food for themselves and their animals. They could also raise hemp and flax, from which they made oil and cloth. Life was not luxurious, but the land gave the Rus everything they needed to live in relative comfort.

The most comfortable places to settle were near rivers. The soil near rivers was better for growing crops. More important, the merchants who traded between Scandinavia in the north and the Byzantine Empire of eastern Europe traveled along the rivers. Living near the rivers gave people access to the goods the merchants carried. The trade routes also provided a good income as residents charged merchants to travel through their territory. So people settled along the trade routes of the Dnieper and Volga Rivers. Their settlements grew into cities, and the cities expanded to become city-states, called principalities.

Novgorod

The first principality in Rus was Novgorod. According to legend, it began as a collection of Slavic tribal groups. The

The fifteenth-century kremlin, or fortress, of Novgorod is the oldest fort in Russia. It is a typical kremlin—a wall around the city with several towers.

groups fought among themselves, but they wanted peace. They turned to the Vikings, who often came from the north to trade with them. They asked the Vikings, whom they called Varangians, to settle in their land, establish order, and rule them. In 862, a Viking chieftain named Rurik accepted the offer. Rurik began a dynasty that ruled in the land of Rus for the next seven hundred years.

The Varangians had a well-trod trade route along the series of waterways stretching from the Baltic Sea to the Black Sea. Rurik built settlements along the river trade route. He built walls around the cities to protect them from the steppe raiders and made the city of Novgorod his capital. Situated close to the Baltic Sea, at the northern end of the great north-south trade route, Novgorod was also very near the forests with their furs, wood, honey, and wax. It was far from the steppes, so it was safe from attack. The city thrived and became a center of trade and culture.

Kievan Rus

Rurik ruled from Novgorod, but his successor, Oleg, moved down the Dnieper River. Some of the trading posts along the lower (southern) Dnieper had been attacked or harassed by nomads to the east. Oleg fought off the nomads and captured these small cities. Among the cities he captured was Kiev.

Oleg liked the location of Kiev, on a hill not far from the Black Sea. Three trade routes passed through Kiev. The

Two Cathedrals of Saint Sophia

Saint Sophia is not really a saint; in fact, she is not a person. Sophia is the Greek word for "wisdom," and the churches of Saint Sophia are dedicated to the Wisdom of God. A sixth-century Church of the Holy Wisdom in Constantinople, the capital of the Byzantine Empire, probably inspired the two cathedrals of Saint Sophia in Russia. The first was completed in 1037 in Kiev by Yaroslav the Wise, the second eight years later by his son, Vladimir of Novgorod, in Novgorod.

continued on the next page

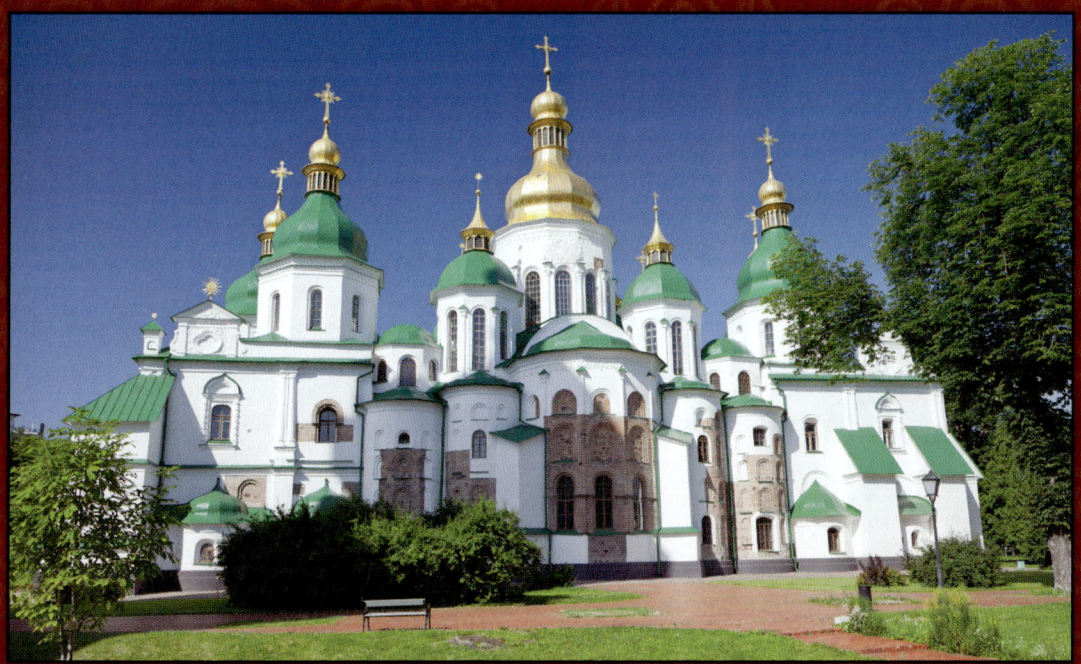

The Saint Sophia Cathedral in Kiev was burned and looted a number of times in its almost ten-century history. Its beautiful and unusual appearance reflects several restorations.

continued from the previous page

Yaroslav built his cathedral in Kiev to celebrate his victory over a confederation of steppe raiders. The huge church had five naves, or gathering areas, and thirteen domes. Its walls and ceiling were covered with magnificent artwork. The prince wanted to show that Kiev was as great and as religious as Byzantium. The cathedral was damaged several times—when rival princes attacked Kiev, when fire ravaged the city, and when the Mongols invaded. It lay in disrepair until the seventeenth century, when it was finally restored to its former glory. That is when the golden, onion-shaped domes were added to the original domes.

After the Russian Revolution of 1917, the anti-religious government wanted to tear the cathedral down. However, many historians in Russia protested. The leaders did not demolish the building, but they refused to permit religious activities in the church. Instead, they turned the building into a museum. Most of the centuries-old artwork was saved, and the Cathedral of Saint Sophia stands today as a reminder of the grandeur of Kievan Rus.

region's climate was warmer and its soil better than in Novgorod. The people of Kiev could grow wheat, corn, sunflowers, sugar beets, and tobacco. Around 880, Oleg moved the capital from Novgorod to Kiev, calling Kiev the "Mother of Rus Cities." He proclaimed himself Prince of Kievan Rus.

Kievan Rus included a number of cities scattered between the Baltic and Black Seas. The Rurikid ruler assigned cities to his brothers, who were considered "princes of the royal

Vladimir the Great brought Orthodox Christianity to Russia. A picture in the fifteenth-century Radziwill Chronicle *depicts Vladimir (top) and his bodyguards (bottom) being baptized.*

blood" because they were related to Rurik. Each city and its surrounding land was therefore a principality ruled by a prince; all were under the Great Prince, who commanded the principality of Kiev. The system was much like that of the Mongol khans.

In Kievan Rus, however, the supreme leader was not elected. The oldest or most able princes were given the biggest and best principalities, and as a prince died, each prince below him "moved up." Theoretically, someone could start with a small principality and advance to become Great Prince. But that was unlikely as several brothers sat between the lowest and highest positions. As with the Mongols, the Rus system bred competition and conflict. Many Rurikid princes died under mysterious circumstances.

Golden Age

The best time—the Golden Age—for Kievan Rus was during the reigns of Vladimir the Great and Yaroslav the Wise. Despite the fighting among the princes, Kievan Rus prospered and grew. Prince Vladimir I (980–1015) built a strong relationship with his biggest trading partner, the Byzantine Empire. He married the sister of the Byzantine emperor, and he ordered Orthodox Christianity, the faith of Byzantium, as the official religion of Kievan Rus.

When Vladimir died, his oldest son killed three of his many brothers so he could become Great Prince of Kiev. The prince of Novgorod went to war against his murderous brother. He won and thus became Yaroslav the Wise (1019–1054).

Yaroslav united the principalities of Novgorod and Kiev, making his realm bigger and more powerful. He also waged a number of successful raids, further enlarging his territory and his fame. To ensure good relationships with other countries, he married his daughters to rulers of Norway, France, and Hungary.

To mark one of his victories, Yaroslav built the magnificent Cathedral of Saint Sophia. He built other churches as well as monasteries. He started schools, commissioned monks to translate books, and furnished a library. He also began writing a law code. Culture and learning reached a high point under his leadership.

Kiev Fractures

However, Yaroslav's successors were not able to hold the empire together. As happened with the Mongols, the different principalities found they did not need one another. They looked at the Great Prince of Kiev as just one of many princes, not their ruler. Shortly after Yaroslav's death, the prince of Vladimir-Suzdal captured and sacked Kiev. The fighting among the princes of the blood continued, and Kievan Rus fell apart into separate principalities.

The principalities had become rich through trade with nations in the west. But raids from nomads in the east

In 1238, Batu Khan besieged the town of Kozelsk for seven weeks and eventually destroyed it. Batu was so angry at the defiance of the defenders that he called Kozelsk the "evil town."

made traveling on the trade routes difficult. Even worse, the Crusaders destroyed Constantinople (Byzantium) in 1204, ruining its trade with Rus and the alliances Rus had in eastern Europe.

By the end of the twelfth century, the principalities' wealth had dried up, their military might had shriveled, and their influence had evaporated. Rus was no longer a strong, prosperous, united empire. It was "easy pickings" for an invading army.

Chapter 3
The Empires Clash

The Mongols first arrived west of the Urals in 1223. After invading Persia, a part of the conquering army continued westward. They came to the Kipchaks, a large nomadic confederation just southeast of Rus. The Kipchaks and Rus were enemies, but the nomads knew they could not fight off the invaders without help. At the same time, some of the Rus princes realized that if the Mongols defeated their neighbors, they would be next. So some of the Rus princes agreed to stand with the Kipchaks against the Mongol army.

At first, opposing the invaders seemed like a smart move. The Rus outnumbered the raiders, and they knew the battleground. When the Rus attacked, the small Mongol force fell back. But the retreat was a feint—a trick, a pretend defeat to draw the Rus into a trap. As the Rus chased the fleeing raiders for days, the exhausted Rus ran straight into a large, fresh Mongol army at the Kalka River. The battle was a terrible defeat for the Rus. Most of their soldiers were brutally killed, and only one prince escaped.

The Real Conquest (1237-1240)

After the battle, the Mongol army left Rus and went back to Asia. But the general who had led the victory, Subutai the Valiant, left spies throughout the cities of Kievan Rus. He planned to return.

Subutai the Valiant (1176–1248)

Many people know Genghis Khan as the fierce warrior who built the largest land empire in history. But few know the name of the general who was the real power behind the ferocious army, Subutai the Valiant. Subutai came to Genghis Khan in his teens, following his older brother. He sought to serve a popular and successful leader.

As the son of a blacksmith, growing up in the forests that bordered the steppe, Subutai was probably not a good horseman or a skilled archer when he offered his services to Genghis Khan. But he was smart and loyal. The teenager learned the ways of the Mongol raider and within ten years, he was commanding some of Genghis Khan's forces to spectacular victories. Subutai's strength was not in charging the enemy but in coming up with clever ways to beat them. His use of spies, siege weapons, and trickery were new to many of the armies he faced. He fought across Asia and Europe, from Korea to Hungary, under four khans: Genghis, Ogedei, Batu, and Guyuk. He commanded his last army at age seventy. Military historians recognize Subutai the Valiant as one of the greatest generals in history.

Four years later, Genghis Khan died, and Batu was soon the leader of what would become the Golden Horde. The new Great Khan, Ogedei, ordered Batu to begin taking territory to his west. He allowed Genghis Khan's best general to command the Golden Horde army. Thus, in 1237, Subutai reappeared at the border of Rus with a Mongol army of 120,000 men.

As Batu and Subutai crossed the Volga River, the first principality they came to was Ryazan. Batu's original plan was not to capture the city but to take from it anything of value. He wanted tribute—protection money. He told the leaders of Ryazan that if they paid what he demanded, he would not attack the principality. His demand was one-tenth of all their weapons and one-tenth of their soldiers for the Mongol army. The prince refused to pay, hoping other Rus princes would help him fend off the intruders. But no one came to his aid in time. Batu crushed the army that defied him, utterly destroyed Ryazan, and continued farther into Rus.

Over the next three years, one principality after another met the same fate. The Mongols were merciless to all who resisted them. They burned cities, took treasures, and ruthlessly killed young and old. Only Novgorod escaped. It was in the far north and surrounded by marsh. Apparently Batu did not think the principality was worth having his army slog through thick mud and heavy rain. About 60 miles (97 km) from the city, he stopped and turned around. He had already captured Kiev, so by 1240, the Golden Horde was in control of almost all of Rus.

Two years later, Batu left the area. The Great Khan had died, and all the khans were required to meet to elect a new leader. This was when the four khanates began to separate. Batu was not selected as the Great Khan, but he remained very powerful. He established the city of Sarai Batu on the lower Volga as the capital of the Golden Horde. He did not go back to conquering territory. Instead, he turned his attention to ruling the lands he had already gained.

THE TATAR YOKE (1240–1480)

Batu Khan and his successors ruled Rus for almost 250 years. Russian historians call this time the "Tatar Yoke." Tatar, also spelled Tartar, is a word sometimes used for the Mongols of the Golden Horde. The Mongols were not Tatars; Tatars were Turkic people of the western steppe conquered by the Mongols. Just as the Golden Horde is sometimes called the Kipchak Khanate because it eventually included many Kipchaks, Russians call the Mongols Tatars because the Golden Horde absorbed many Tatars. The term "yoke" refers to the wooden frame clamped on the necks of oxen to control them and force them to work. That is how Russians see this period of their history: a foreign power oppressing them miserably.

Before Mongols (on horses) put their captives in their armies, they forced them to parade with yokes around their necks — forked wooden sticks closed with iron bars.

As oppressive as the Tatar Yoke was, Mongol rule in Rus was less severe than in other parts of the khanates. On the steppes, the Mongols took over all they conquered. They spread out over the land and killed, scattered, or enslaved the people. Everyone they defeated became part of their empire so that the tribes no longer existed as separate people. However, the Rus cities had no grass for their cattle, and the Mongols did not need any more land. The only things the Rus had that interested the Mongols were money and people. The khans could take those without occupying their cities and slaughtering all the inhabitants. So they ruled indirectly, allowing the princes to keep their positions as long as they did what the khans told them.

One thing the khans ordered them was to pay tribute. They decided how much to tax each principality by taking a census—a count—of all the citizens. The count also told them how many men the prince had to give to the Mongol army. The princes were forced to supply people for Mongol projects, such as building roads, bridges, and postal stations. Crops grown in Rus went to feed Mongol armies and their horses.

The Mongols controlled who could be prince of a Rus city. They issued yarlyks, which were like licenses. These gave the princes permission to rule. To renew the yarlyks, princes were required to go to the Golden Horde capital and bow down to the khan, with their foreheads touching the ground, and pledge their loyalty. Sometimes they had to go even farther, to the capital city of the Great Khan in Mongolia. Thus, for the two and a half centuries of Mongol domination, the Golden Horde humiliated, robbed, and oppressed the Rus.

Alexander Nevsky (1236-1263)

The man Russians revere as their greatest hero lived at the beginning of the Tatar Yoke. He was named Alexander Yaroslavich, meaning Alexander, the son of (vich) Yaroslav. His father was the Prince of Kiev when the Mongols invaded. By that time, Kiev was not as important a city as Vladimir. Yaroslav bowed to Batu Khan and asked to be assigned to Vladimir. Batu agreed and named him Yaroslav II, Grand Prince of Vladimir. He was basically the ruler—under the khan—of all of Rus.

Yaroslav's son, Alexander, was Prince of Novgorod when the Mongols came to Rus. Batu Khan did not burn and plunder Novgorod as he did the rest of Rus, but he did demand tribute from the city. Alexander knew what had happened to the other cities, and he had a choice. Should he fight the forces that had swallowed up everything before them? Or should he submit to their rule so his city and its people would be spared?

He chose submission. Some think he did so to enjoy the power the Mongols offered, but most believe he acted out of concern for his subjects. As long as the cities paid the tribute, the khans would leave them alone. Alexander delivered the taxes, so the Mongols left Novgorod to itself.

But problems came from the west. European countries, thinking all the armies of Rus were busy fighting the Golden

This early eighteenth-century painting depicts Alexander Nevsky as a prince (symbolized by the crown), a warrior (sword), and a saint (halo encircling his head).

Horde, attacked Novgorod. Alexander was only nineteen when the first invasion came. He repelled the Swedes at the Neva River, earning the nickname "Nevsky" ("of the Neva"). Two years later, he defeated the German Teutonic Knights at the Battle of the Ice, fought on a frozen river.

After his father died, Alexander made several visits to the Golden Horde in Sarai. In 1252, the khan appointed him Grand Prince of Vladimir. In that position, he tried to protect all of Rus from any Mongol anger. When residents of a city revolted against the Mongol census and taxation, Alexander stopped the protest so the Mongols would not punish them. He collected the tribute money himself so Mongol census takers would not treat the people harshly. His cooperation with the Golden Horde may have saved Rus from annihilation. For this and his many military victories—and perhaps because he became a monk at the end of his life—the Russian Orthodox Church declared him a saint.

Under the Tatar Yoke, the principalities had some freedoms denied many others. Because the princes still ruled their cities, they continued to compete with one another for the better positions. It would be another century after Alexander Nevsky before one principality was strong enough to challenge the Golden Horde.

Chapter 4
A Winner Emerges

When Alexander Nevsky died, his youngest son, Daniel, was only two. So the young boy inherited the smallest and poorest of his father's properties. It was just a tiny town within the principality of Vladimir-Suzdal (the two cities were joined under one prince). Little more than an outpost of Suzdal on the Moskva River, it was called Moscow.

While Daniel's brothers and uncles fought for control of the largest and most prosperous cities, especially Vladimir, Daniel concentrated on enlarging his realm. As cities in neighboring principalities were torn apart by rival princes and forgotten, Daniel added them to his lands. One of Daniel's uncles, who had no sons, left his city to Daniel when he died. Thus the tiny outpost of Moscow grew little by little into a sizeable principality that also became known as Muscovy.

The growing principality attracted the interest of its closest neighbor, the Prince of Ryazan. In their feuds over power and territory, the princes sometimes enlisted the help of the khans against rival cities. The Prince of Ryazan, with the aid of forces from the Golden Horde, attacked Moscow in 1300. To everyone's surprise, Daniel drove the attackers back.

Daniel's action was the first Rus victory over a Mongol army since the Golden Horde first appeared on the western steppe almost eighty years before. The Mongol force was small, and the battle was brief, but the action was still a success for the Prince of Moscow. For people who had been under the humiliating oppression of the Tatar Yoke for more than sixty years,

A monument to Prince Daniel erected in Moscow in 1997 shows the saint, known for pursuing peace, holding a church in one hand and a sheathed sword in the other.

any defeat of their enemy, no matter how small, was a hopeful sign. Perhaps the yoke could be overthrown.

Great Location

Despite Daniel's victory, Moscow seemed the least likely of the principalities to rid Rus of the Golden Horde. It was quite small in comparison with the others. Its prince was from the royal line of Rurik, but his branch of the royal line was a minor one. Still, Moscow had an important advantage over the other cities.

Its greatest advantage was its location. Moscow was in northwestern Rus, surrounded by other Rus principalities. Any invaders, from the steppe or from Europe, would come to other cities before they reached Moscow. Forests to the north and the Oka River to the south were natural barriers to attacking forces. So Moscow escaped the worst of the frequent warfare that plagued all of Rus. The city grew as people in other principalities fled to the relative safety of Moscow.

Moscow's location also gave it an economic advantage. Situated where two rivers came together and flowed into the Volga, it was on the important trade route from Novgorod to the Black Sea. Because the goods that passed through Moscow ended up in Byzantium, the princes of Muscovy developed a good relationship with the Byzantine Empire. The Byzantine Empire was the center of the Orthodox Church, and the Orthodox Church was very important to many of the people and most of the rulers of Rus. In 1326, the Metropolitan

This painting of Moscow during Ivan I's reign shows one of the rivers bordering the city, the oak wall Ivan built, and the spires of several churches he erected.

Coats of Arms of Russia

A coat of arms is a set of symbols, usually on a shield, that represent a family, city, state, or country. It was originally embroidered on a soldier's tunic (coat) that he wore over his armor (arms). The coat of arms of modern Russia has evolved over the centuries, with changing symbols reflecting the country's history. Historians have different ideas of what the symbols mean.

The double eagle has been associated with Russia at least since the fifteenth century. Some think that because the double eagle was also used by the Byzantine Empire, the Russian rulers wanted to say they were the heirs of that empire and thus also of the Roman Empire. Others say the heads, facing east and west, declare that Russia is the center of world power and culture. The three crowns may represent the three khanates conquered by Ivan IV. The orb and the scepter in the eagle's claws are symbols of a monarchy. At one time the eagle held swords and thunderbolts instead, suggesting military greatness.

In the center of Russia's coat of arms is the coat of arms of Moscow, symbolizing that the

Moscow's first coat of arms pictured St. George. After the Bolshevik Revolution of 1917, Russian abolished this image and all the old symbols. It was restored in 1993.

Russian Empire rose from the Principality of Muscovy. The image depicts the popular legend of St. George, the patron saint of Prince Yuri, slaying a dragon. According to the story, a dragon terrorized an ancient pagan Rus village. When George heroically killed the dragon, the villagers accepted Christianity. Many years later, the Russian Orthodox Church declared George a saint, and Dmitri Donskoy made him the patron saint of Moscow.

(head) of the Orthodox Church in Rus moved from Kiev to Moscow, making Moscow seem very important.

THE PRINCES AND THE KHAN

The real power in Rus, however, was not the Church or any prince; it was the khan of the Golden Horde. Uzbek Khan (1313–1341) boasted an army of three hundred thousand—more than enough to keep the principalities in line. He ruled all of Rus from his capital of Serai on the Volga River, appointing and executing princes as he wished.

One of the princes to whom the khan took a liking was Daniel's son Yuri. Uzbek allowed Yuri to marry his sister and gave him the yarlyk to be Grand Prince of Vladimir (in addition to Prince of Moscow), the most powerful position in Rus. The khan executed Yuri's chief rivals, but not before one of them murdered Yuri. The title of Prince of Moscow fell to Yuri's brother, Ivan.

Ivan I (1328–1340) followed Yuri's example, maintaining his loyalty to Uzbek Khan. The Mongol overlord granted Ivan the yarlyk of Grand Prince of Vladimir. His job was to collect the taxes and tribute from all the principalities of Rus and deliver them to the khan. Knowing that fulfilling that responsibility would keep him in power, Ivan performed well. He earned the name Kalita, which means "Moneybags."

He was a "moneybag" for the Golden Horde but also for Muscovy. Ivan used the wealth of his position to expand his territory. He purchased land around Moscow. He lent money to other principalities, and when the principalities could not pay the loans back, he added their cities to his. He encouraged people to move to Moscow and made it a very safe place to live and work. This activity earned him another name: "Gatherer of the Russian Lands."

The Horde Weakens

At the same time Moscow was growing in size and strength, the Golden Horde was beginning to show signs of weakening. The Horde reached the peak of its power under Uzbek Khan, but his vast empire was difficult to rule. The sub-khans in charge of different parts of the far-flung empire fought among themselves.

Occasionally, some of the conquered people would rebel, and an army would have to put down the revolt. The Mongols were no longer nomadic herdsmen. They had settled into cities and relied on the tribute from their subjects to sustain their lifestyles. They could not simply burn rebellious towns and kill all their inhabitants as they had in the past. They needed the people to work and pay taxes. The khans found governing more difficult than conquering.

However, the real enemy that sapped the strength of the Golden Horde was not infighting, a foreign army, or a local uprising. The real enemy was an army of fleas. In the mid-fourteenth century, rats with rat fleas joined the caravans that carried trade goods across the steppe and into Europe. The rats carried bubonic plague, then called the Black Death, and the fleas spread the disease from the rats to humans. Historians estimate that the Black Death wiped out more than half of all the people in the affected areas—perhaps as many as seventy-five million people.

The weakness of the Golden Horde was very obvious in 1359, when the khan was assassinated by his brother. For more than twenty years, the khanate was in complete disarray. One person after another claimed the throne, only to be overthrown by the next strong man. When two Mongol generals, each declaring himself the khan, both demanded tribute, the Grand Prince of Moscow and Vladimir saw his chance to rid Rus of the Tatar Yoke.

Muscovy Flexes Its Muscles

The Grand Prince at the time was Dmitri II (1359–1389), grandson of Ivan Kalita. While the Horde was disintegrating into bloody family squabbles, Dmitri continued his grandfather's

Dmitri II (with halo, later proclaimed a saint) leads Russian armies into battle at Kulikovo Field. Dmitri was badly wounded, and twelve Russian princes died in the battle.

mission of gathering the Rus lands. He enlarged the Principality of Moscow through battles or treaties with other principalities. He built the first kremlin in Moscow—a stone fortress ("kremlin" means "fortress") that would protect the city from invading armies.

In 1380, Dmitri decided that Muscovy was big enough and strong enough to challenge Mongol control. On behalf of all Rus, he refused to collect the tribute. In effect, he was proclaiming that Rus was an independent state, no longer subject to the Golden Horde.

One of the generals who claimed to be the khan, Mamai, accepted the challenge. He charged toward Moscow with a huge Mongol army. By this time all but two of the Rus principalities were allied with Muscovy. Their combined forces, however, totaled about half what Mamai had. Even though badly outnumbered, Dmitri led his army into battle at Kulikovo Field, just across the Don River.

When the entire army was on the field, Dmitri untied the boats that had carried them across the river, letting them drift away. His soldiers had no way to retreat; it was win or die for them. Many, many died in the lopsided battle, but the determined Rus army won. Mamai was forced to withdraw.

The Battle of Kulikovo was a huge victory for Moscow's prince. From then on, he was known as Dmitri Donsky ("of the Don") for his magnificent feat near the River Don. The battle was the first joint venture of so many Rus principalities. It cemented Muscovy as the leader. And it marked the first significant defeat of the Golden Horde by the armies of Rus.

A Century Later

But the great victory did not end Mongol control over Rus. The other general who claimed to be the khan, Tokhtamysh, defeated Mamai and took charge of his army. Two years after the Battle of Kulikovo, Tokhtamysh took revenge on Moscow, burning it to the ground. He forced Dmitri to pledge loyalty to him. Rus went back to paying tribute to the Golden Horde.

Still, the people took courage from the battle's outcome. They knew now that the khans could be defeated. And they understood that they could win only if the principalities worked together as one. It would take a hundred years before they had another chance to challenge their enemy. During those years, the Princes of Moscow managed to further enlarge both their land and their power. By the time of Ivan III, the Great (1462–1505), all of Rus was united under the leadership of Moscow.

The Golden Horde, on the other hand, had dissolved into several separate khanates. A Mongol warrior named Timur, or Tamerlane, establishing his own empire on the western steppe, had invaded and split the Horde. One by one, Kazan, Crimea, Astrakhan, and Siberia broke off and became independent khanates. By 1466, the remaining area was simply called the "Great Horde." But it was not so great that Ivan III would not challenge its rule over Rus. In 1480, Ivan did not deliver the tribute.

In response, Akhmat Khan gathered an army and advanced toward Moscow, stopping at the Ugra River. Ivan also amassed an army and stood with his men on the other side of the river.

A Rus Republic

Novgorod was unique among the principalities of Rus. It was not only the first city of the Rurikid dynasty, but it was also a republic, a city governed by the people. It gained its unusual status under Yaroslav the Wise. In Kievan Rus, Novgorod was second in importance to Kiev. When the Prince of Kiev died, the Prince of Novgorod was expected to advance to his position. However, in the bloody family squabbles that followed Vladimir the Great's death, Yaroslav—who was the Prince of Novgorod and therefore should become the prince of Kiev—had to fight for four years for the "throne" of Kiev. Because the people of Novgorod helped him win the crown, he rewarded them by granting the city many special privileges. One was the right to choose its own prince. From 1136 on, an assembly of citizens actually ruled the city, electing princes they liked and ousting ones they disliked. Novgorod remained fiercely independent, fending off nearly all attempts at outside control, until finally brought under Moscow by Ivan IV.

Akhmat expected reinforcements to join him, but they did not come. While Ivan waited, Akmat eventually withdrew without much of a fight. The "battle" was called the Great Standoff at the River Ugra. It signaled the end of Mongol domination of Rus. No more tribute was paid. The standoff marked the end of the 240-year Tatar Yoke.

CHAPTER 5
A New Empire

Ivan the Great threw the Tatar Yoke off Rus, but he did not destroy the Mongols. Nor did he dampen their greed. None of the broken pieces of the Golden Horde was powerful enough to pry tribute from Rus or to impose their rule, but they did not leave their former subjects alone. For another hundred years the remaining khanates attacked Rus principalities repeatedly. Their goal was to take possessions and slaves. They often burned the cities they looted.

The worst of the attackers was the Crimean Khanate. Crimea had absorbed the Great Horde and conducted a thriving slave trade with the Ottoman Empire, which had replaced Byzantium. At least once a year the khan invaded Rus and captured people for its slave market. In 1571, a Crimean army sacked Moscow. The soldiers carried off all the sacred treasures of the monasteries, seized the merchants' wares, and set the city on fire. The only structure that survived was the stone kremlin.

From Rus to Russia

The prince of Moscow at that time was Ivan IV, the Terrible (1533–1584). He saw himself in the same

The khan and other leaders of Kazan surrender to nineteen-year-old Ivan the Terrible after the Russian army captured the capital city of the Kazan Khanate.

way other princes of Muscovy had envisioned themselves: as the ruler of all Rus. He was able to bring all the principalities under the domination of Moscow, and in 1547, he had himself crowned tsar, the first prince to take that title. The word is the Russian form of "caesar," and it means "emperor."

Ivan was called "the Terrible" for good reason. He was ruthless in bringing all the Rus principalities and nobles under his control. Plots, murders, and conspiracies were common, and Ivan was suspicious of everyone. If he thought a particular boyar, or noble, was against him, he would have him fiendishly tortured and publically executed. Many hundreds of boyars were killed in this way, often with their entire families. When Ivan believed someone in Novgorod betrayed him, he led an army against the principality. He looted and ravaged small towns, devastated the main city, set fire to crops growing in the fields, and butchered thousands of men, women, and children. He created a police force that terrorized boyars and peasants alike. Dressed in black and riding black horses, the force rooted out and punished all dissent. Ivan even killed his own son in an angry outburst.

But despite the tsar's cruelty and the terrible amount of blood he shed, Ivan IV ruled a united Rus. He was determined to make his realm into an empire. Some church leaders in Rus had suggested that Moscow was the third Rome. They said the Roman Empire was the first great empire to rise on the earth and the Byzantine Empire was the second. Byzantium, founded by the Roman emperor Constantine as the Roman Empire in the West was dying, had long been called the Eastern Roman Empire. It had been thought of as the protector of the Orthodox Church. When the Ottomans destroyed Byzantium in 1453, some in Rus pictured Moscow as the defender of the church and of culture—the third Rome. Whether or not Ivan believed the theory, he did believe he could build an empire.

His first step was to beef up his military. He made agreements with the Cossacks, nomadic herders and raiders on his southern border, to defend that border for Rus. Then he went after the khanates that had splintered off the Golden Horde. When he conquered the Kazan Khanate in 1552, it was the first Rus takeover of territory outside the principalities. Two other khanates also fell to Ivan's army: Astrakhan and Siberia. All that remained of the Mongol Empire was the Khanate of Crimea. There, Ivan was unsuccessful; Crimea would remain a thorn to Rus for another 180 years.

After his victories in the east, Ivan turned west, to Europe. He tried to win for Rus a port on the Baltic Sea. But he had little chance against the armies of Lithuania, Denmark, Sweden, and Poland. However, the nations of Europe took notice of this new power. It entered the history books by its European name: Russia.

A New Dynasty

Ivan not only failed to conquer any territory in Europe, but he also left his empire a mess. Russia spiraled downward into

During the Time of Troubles, the people of Moscow revolted. The leaders put down the rebellions harshly, even setting Moscow on fire.

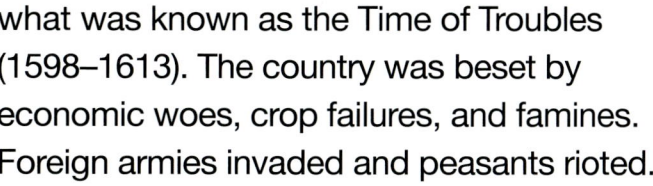

what was known as the Time of Troubles (1598–1613). The country was beset by economic woes, crop failures, and famines. Foreign armies invaded and peasants rioted.

During the turmoil, the country was without a leader. Ivan's son had died without an heir in 1598, bringing the line of Rurik to an end. The dynasty that had ruled Rus for more than seven hundred years had no more sons. But many people wanted to be tsar. A number came forward, claiming to be some relative of Ivan's. Some managed to rule briefly, but in a climate of lies, arrests, betrayals, and assassinations, none lasted long.

Finally, a group of boyars called a Council of the Land in 1613 to try to find a leader who would put an end to the chaos. They agreed upon a distant relative of the Ruriks, a grandson of Ivan the Terrible's first wife, named Michael Romanov. He was only sixteen, but others in his family would help him learn to govern. When he was crowned tsar in 1613, he began the Romanov dynasty, which would rule Russia for three centuries.

Under the Romanovs, Russia grew in size and standing in the world. Russia was behind Europe in a number of ways, but

In 1787 Catherine the Great toured the new lands she had annexed to Russia. Here she is pictured riding into one of the cities of Crimea.

Peter the Great (1689–1725) instituted many changes, making the country more like the European nations. He had himself crowned Emperor of All Russia in 1721, officially proclaiming that Russia was an empire. Catherine the Great (1762–1796) continued to add western lands to the empire. In 1783, she was able to take over Crimea, finally extinguishing the last of the khanates of the Golden Horde.

The Golden Horde had dominated what is today Russia for almost 250 years. The Russian Empire lasted nearly as long— about two hundred years. But it too came to an end, brought down by the Bolshevik Revolution of 1917. Throughout history, kingdoms and dynasties rise and fall. Few have stood as long, been as large, or had so great an impact on the world as the Mongol and Russian empires of Eurasia.

Glossary

assimilate Become absorbed into.

boyar Russian noble.

Byzantine Empire The remains of the Roman Empire after most of the empire disintegrated in the fifth century. Also called the Eastern Roman Empire, it was located in eastern Europe and lasted until 1453. Its capital, Byzantium, became Constantinople.

caravan Group of people and vehicles traveling together on a journey.

confederation One group made up of several people, tribes, or countries that join together for a common purpose.

horde Among Mongols and other central Asian nomads, a clan or tribal group. The term has come to mean a large group of people, especially an army.

khan Among Mongols and some other central Asian peoples, a ruler of a tribe, a tribal confederation, or some geographic area.

khanate Territory ruled by a khan.

kurultai Council meeting of Mongol clan leaders.

marsh Land that is wet and soft, usually very muddy or swamp-like.

Metropolitan In Eastern Orthodox churches, the leader of the church in a city or region, similar to a bishop.

nomad Person who has no permanent home and moves to different locations.

principality Territory ruled by a prince.

Rus Name of the people and land of Russia from the ninth to the sixteenth century.

sack To loot, or steal goods from, a city or other place after attacking it.

steppe Large tract of semi-arid grassland located in central Asia and southeastern Europe that is generally flat and without trees.

subject Person who is under the rule of someone else.

successor Person who comes after another and has the title or authority the first one had.

tribute Money or some other valuable that one country pays to another in return for the more powerful country promising to protect the weaker country from attack.

yarlyk A decree issued by a Mongol khan, especially a decree that granted a prince authority to rule a principality.

For More Information

Indo-Mongolian Society
PO Box 491
New York, NY 10156
Website: http://www.mongolianculture.com
The Indo-Mongolian Society was founded in 1990 to share the history of Mongolia, central Asia, the Mongol peoples, and related cultures. Its website contains a wealth of information on these topics, as well as lists of resources for further exploration.

Moscow State Historical Museum
1 Red Square
Moscow 103012
Russia
Website: http://www.moscow.info/museums/state-historical-museum.aspx
The Moscow State Historical Museum opened in 1894. It contains objects and information from every era of Russia's history from ancient to modern times.

Museum of Russian Art
5500 Stevens Avenue S
Minneapolis, MN 55419
(612) 821-9045
Website: http://tmora.org
The Museum of Russian Art contains art and artifacts from throughout Russian history. In addition to the art and changing exhibits, the museum offers online exhibitions that feature

text and photographs about various periods of Russian history.

Museum of Russian Icons
203 Union Street
Clinton, MA 01510
(978) 598-5000
Website: http://museumofrussianicons.org/en
The Museum of Russian Icons houses icons and other religious objects of the Russian Orthodox faith dating from 988. The museum holds special events for children and families and has a large collection of videos and reading material.

State Hermitage Museum
Palace Square, 2
St. Petersburg 190000
Russia
Website: http://www.hermitagemuseum.org
Once the Winter Palace and other buildings of the tsars, the State Hermitage Museum was founded by Catherine the Great and houses her art collection, as well as millions of other art pieces from around the world. Its website describes the buildings, collections, and exhibits and lists videos and other resources.

Victoria and Albert Museum
Cromwell Road
London SW7 2RL
United Kingdom
Website: http://www.vam.ac.uk
The Victoria and Albert Museum displays clothing, jewelry, furniture, and many other types of artifacts from Russia. The items,

together with explanations and additional information, can be viewed online.

Websites

Because of the changing nature of Internet links, Rosen Publishing has developed an online list of websites related to the subject of this book. This site is updated regularly. Please use this link to access the list:

http://www.rosenlinks.com/MON/gold

For Further Reading

Baumer, Christopher. *The History of Central Asia: The Age of the Steppe Warrior*. New York, NY: Taurus and Co., 2012.

Carpini, Giovani DiPlano. *The Story of the Mongols Whom We Call the Tartars*. 2nd ed. Translated by Erik Hildinger. Wellesley, MA: Branden Books, 2014.

Curtin, Jeremiah. *The Mongols in Russia*. 1908. Reprint. San Diego, CA: Didactic, 2015.

Dittmar, Brian. *Mongol Warriors*. Minneapolis, MN: Bellwether Media, 2012.

Dole, Nathan. *The Story of Russia*. 1895. Reprint. San Diego, CA: Didactic, 2013.

Duffy, James P., and Vincent L. Ricci. *The Czars*. Alameda, CA: New World City, 2015.

Fleming, Candace. *The Family Romanov: Murder, Rebellion, and the Fall of Imperial Russia*. New York, NY: Schwartz and Wade, 2014.

Matthews, Rupert. *Mongols*. New York, NY: Gareth Stevens, 2015.

Sepahban, Lois. *Mongol Warriors*. Mankato, MN: Child's World, 2015.

Bibliography

Bartlett, Roger. *A History of Russia*. New York, NY: Palgrave Macmillan, 2005.

Gabriel, Richard A. *Genghis Khan's Greatest General: Subotai the Valiant*. Norman, OK: University of Oklahoma Press, 2006.

Grousset, Rene. *The Empire of the Steppes: A History of Central Asia*. New Brunswick, NJ: Rutgers University Press, 1970.

Hosking, Geoffrey. *Russia and the Russians: A History*. Cambridge, MA: Harvard University Press, 2001.

Karasulas, Antony. *Mounted Archers of the Steppe 600 BC to 1300 AD*. Oxford, England: Osprey, 2004.

Michell, Robert. *The Chronicle of Novgorod: 1016-1471*. Translated by Neville Forbes. London, England: Office of the Society, 1914.

Moscow City Government. "Coat of Arms of Moscow." Retrieved December 10, 2015 (http://www.old.mos.ru/en/about/symbols/blazon).

National Geographic Encyclopedia. "Yurt." Retrieved November 23, 2015 (http://education.nationalgeographic.org/encyclopedia/yurt).

Ukraine Truth. "Rename Russia by Its Primary Historical Term 'Muscovy,' Some Ukrainians Suggest." October 19, 2014 (http://ukraine-truth.com/2014/10/rename-russia-primary-historical-term-muscovy-ukrainians-suggest).

Unku, Alexey. "Russia and the Double-headed Eagle." Victoria and Albert Museum. Retrieved December 10, 2015 (http://www.vam.ac.uk/content/articles/r/russia-double-headed-eagle).

INDEX

A
Akhmat Khan, 46, 47
Alexander Nevsky, 33–35, 36
Altai Mountains, 6

B
Baltic Sea, 20, 22, 51
Batu Khan, 13, 15, 29, 30, 31, 33
Black Death, 43
Black Sea, 20, 22, 38
Blue Horde, 13, 15
Bolshevik Revolution of 1917, 54
boyars, 50, 53
bubonic plague, 43
Byzantine Empire, 18, 21, 22, 24, 27, 38, 40, 48, 50–51

C
Catherine the Great, 54
census, 32, 35
Chagatai Khanate, 11
Church of the Holy Wisdom, 21
coats of arms, Russian, 40–41
confederations, 8, 9, 22, 28
Constantine, 50
Constantinople, 21, 27
Cossacks, 51
Council of the Land, 53
Crimean Khanate, 46, 48, 51, 54
Crusaders, 27

D
Daniel Nevsky, 36, 38, 41
Dmitri II, 41, 43, 45, 46
Dnieper River, 18, 20
Don River, 45

G
Genghis Khan, 8, 9, 11, 13, 15, 16, 29, 30
Gobi Desert, 6
Great Khan, 11, 13, 29, 30, 32
Great Prince of Kiev, 24–25
Great Standoff at the River Ugra, 47
Guyuk, 29

I
Ice, Battle of the, 35
Il-Khanate, 11
Ivan I, 41–42, 43
Ivan III, the Great, 46, 48
Ivan IV, the Terrible, 40, 47, 48, 50, 51, 53

K
Kalka River, 28
Kazan Khanate, 28, 51
Kiev, 20–25, 28, 33, 41, 47
    Golden Age, 24–25
Kipchaks, 15, 28, 31
kremlin, 45, 48
Kulikovo, Battle of, 45, 46
kurultai, 11

M
Mamai, 45, 46
Metropolitan, 38, 41
Moskva River, 36

N
Neva River, 35
Novgorod, 18–20, 21, 22, 30, 33, 38, 47, 50

Index

O
Ogedei, 11, 15, 29
Oka River, 38
Oleg, 20, 22
Orda, 13
Orthodox Christianity, 24, 38, 51
Ottoman Empire, 48, 51

P
People of the Felt Tents, 12–13
Peter the Great, 54

R
Roman Empire, 40, 50
Romanov, Michael, 53
Romanov dynasty, 53
Rurik, 20, 22, 24, 47, 53
Russian Orthodox Church, 35, 41
Russian Revolution of 1917, 22, 54
Ryazan, 30, 36

S
Saint George, legend of, 41
Saint Sophia, cathedrals of, 21–22, 25
Sarai Batu, 30, 35
Subutai the Valient, 28, 29, 30

T
Tatar Yoke, 31–33, 35, 36, 43, 47, 48
Temujin, 9
Teutonic Knights, 35
Time of Troubles, 53
Timur, 46
Tokhtamysh, 46
tsars, 50, 53
Turks, 8, 15, 31

U
Ugra River, 46, 47
Ural Mountains, 15, 16, 28
Uzbek Khan, 41, 42

V
Varangians, 20
Vikings, 20
Vladimir of Novgorod, 21, 24, 47
Vladimir-Suzdal, 25, 36
Volga River, 18, 30, 38, 41

W
White Horde, 13, 15

Y
yarlyks, 32, 41, 42
Yaroslav II, 33
Yaroslav the Wise, 21, 22, 24, 25, 33, 47
Yuan dynasty, 11
Yuri Nevsky, 41, 42
yurts, 12–13

About the Author

Ann Byers is a teacher, editor, and writer. She has a degree in history and loves researching and learning about people and events of the past. She has written several books on American and European history. She has visited the sites of Russian exploration on the California coast, but this is her first book on Asia and Russia.

Photo Credits

Cover, p. 3 (Batu Kahn portrait) ullstein bild/Getty Images; cover, p. 3 (map) © iStockphoto.com/Whiteway; interior pages background image (landscape) © iStockphoto.com/joyt; p. 7 hecke61/Shutterstock.com; p. 10 DEA/M. Seemuller/De Agostini/Getty Images; p. 12 Dmitry Chulov/Shutterstock.com; p. 14 Rainer Lesniewski/Shutterstock.com; p. 17 MikeNG/Shutterstock.com; p. 19 DEA/W. Buss/De Agostini/Getty Images; p. 21 vvoe/Shutterstock.com; p. 23 Heritage Images/Hulton Archive/Getty Images; p. 27 Sputnik/Bridgeman Images; p. 30 Pictures from History/Bridgeman Images; pp. 32, 38 Sovfoto/Universal Images Group/Getty Images; p. 36 © Joeri De Rocker/Alamy Stock Photo; p. 40 Atlaspix/Shutterstock.com; pp. 43, 48, 50 Heritage Images/Hulton Fine Art Collection/Getty Images; p. 52 Bibliotheque Nationale, Paris, France/Bridgeman Images

Designer: Matt Cauli; Editor: Meredith Day; Photo Researcher: Nicole DiMella